Greetings, chickens!

MARVELS ANIMALS 47

CHICKENS

KATE RIGGS

CREATIVE EDUCATION | CREATIVE PAPERBACKS

HEY, LET'S START LAYING SOME EGGS!

table of contents

Published by Creative Education and Creative Paperbacks
P.O. Box 227, Mankato, Minnesota 56002
Creative Education and Creative Paperbacks
are imprints of The Creative Company
www.thecreativecompany.us

Design by Wyeth Morgan
Art direction by Blue Design, Inc. (www.bluedes.com)

Images by Getty Images/narvikk, 3, 20–21, THEPALMER, 10–11; iStock/SimplyCreativePhotography, 17; Pexels/Brett Jordan, 4, Ellie Burgin, 1, freestockpro, 6–7, Pixabay, 16, Quang Nguyen Vinh, 14–15, Samer Daboul, 2; Shutterstock/Jugkit tanakittachakorn, 18–19; Unsplash/Brooke Cagle, 8–9, Europeana, cover (middle), Jan Baborák, 13, Jordan Whitt, cover (right), Steven Van Elk, 24, Zachariah Smith, 23; Wikimedia Commons/public domain, cover (left)

Library of Congress Cataloging-in-Publication Data
Names: Riggs, Kate, author.
Title: Chickens / Kate Riggs.
Other titles: Chickens (Marvels)
Description: Mankato, Minnesota : Creative Education/Creative Paperbacks,[2026] | Series: Marvels | Includes bibliographical references and index. | Audience: Ages 4-7 | Audience: Grades K-1 | Summary: "An introduction to chickens, this beginning reader features eye-catching photographs, humorous captions, and basic life science facts about these friendly domestic birds. Includes a labeled image guide, glossary, and further resources"– Provided by publisher.
Identifiers: LCCN 2024044739 (print) | LCCN 2024044740 (ebook) | ISBN 9798889894988 (library binding) | ISBN 9781682777039 (paperback) | ISBN 9798889895787 (ebook)
Subjects: LCSH: Chickens–Juvenile literature.
Classification: LCC SF487.5 .R546 2026 (print) | LCC SF487.5 (ebook) | DDC 636.5–dc23/eng/20241213
LC record available at https://lccn.loc.gov/2024044739
LC ebook record available at https://lccn.loc.gov/2024044740

Printed in India

ERM...WHAT THE OAT?

Feathered chickens are birds. They may be brown, white, black, yellow, or other colors.

A soft **comb** is on top of the head. Flaps of skin hang below the **beak**.

THE SKIN BELOW A CHICKEN'S BEAK IS CALLED A WATTLE.

Chickens scratch at food on the ground. They eat seeds and grains. Sometimes they eat bugs, too.

BUG!
NO BUG!

HENS LAY ABOUT 1 EGG EVERY 24 TO 36 HOURS.

A hen lays eggs in a nest. Baby chicks come out of the eggs. The chicks follow their mother.

Chickens peck at food. They cluck and call to each other. Hens lay eggs.

COCK-A-DOODLE-DOO!

Farewell, chickens!

[Picture a Chicken]

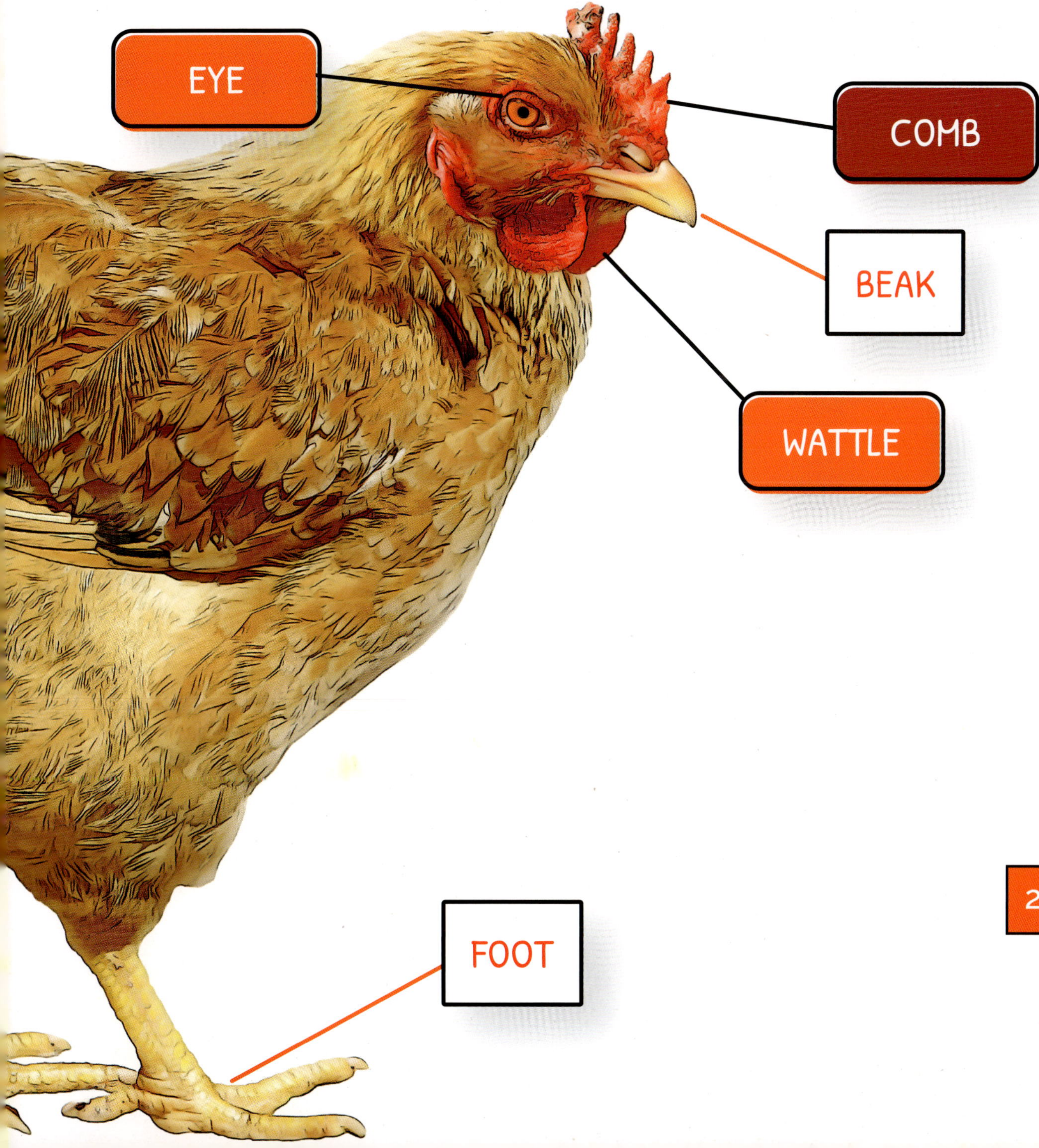
EYE
COMB
BEAK
WATTLE
FOOT

WORDS TO KNOW

beak: the hard front part of a bird's mouth

comb: the fleshy, ridged part that sticks up from the top of a chicken's head

hen: a female chicken that lays eggs

READ MORE

Anderhagen, Anna. *Chicks: A First Look.* Minneapolis: Lerner Publications, 2025.

Rathburn, Betsy. *Chickens*. Minneapolis: Bellwether Media, 2024.

WEBSITES

All about Chickens for Kids and Teachers
https://kiddyhouse.com/themes/farm-animals/chickens/

Learn about types of chickens and how to care for them.

Britannica Kids: Chicken
https://kids.britannica.com/kids/article/chicken/352949o

Find out more about chickens.

INDEX